LGBTQ: A SEXUAL ORIENTATION

Knowledge on same-sex relationship

Mercy Crowns

DEDICATION

This book is dedicated to the woman of my dreams.Thank you Sunshine

TABLE OF CONTENTS

INTRODUCTION

The American Psychological Association has been urging psychologists to lead the charge in eradicating the stigma of mental illness that has long been connected to lesbian, gay, and bisexual orientations. This call to action dates back to 1975. The field of psychology is concerned with the security of individuals and groups, as well as the dangers to that security. Lesbian, homosexual, and bisexual people frequently face prejudice and discrimination, which has been demonstrated to have a negative psychological impact. The purpose of this brochure is to accurately enlighten anyone who wish to learn more about sexual orientation and the effects of prejudice and discrimination on lesbians.

CHAPTER ONE

What is sexual orientation?

An ongoing pattern of emotional, romantic, and/or sexual attraction to either men or women, or both sexes, is referred to as sexual orientation. A person's sense of identity based on these attractions, associated behaviours, and membership in a group of people who share these attractions is sometimes referred to as sexual orientation. A continuum of sexual orientation, from exclusive attraction to the same sex to exclusive attraction to the other sex, has been found over decades of research. However, sexual orientation is typically described in terms of three categories: heterosexual (having romantic or sexual feelings for people of the other sex), gay or lesbian (having feelings for people of the same sex), and bisexual (having emotional, romantic or sexual attractions to both men and women).Many different civilizations and countries around the world have described this range of actions and attractions. Those who exhibit these attractions are described using identity labels throughout many cultures. Lesbians (women attracted to women), gay men (men attracted to men), and bisexuals are the terms used most frequently in the United States (men or women attracted to both sexes). Some individuals, however, might employ several labels or none at all.

Other aspects of sex and gender, such as biological sex (the physical, physiological, and genetic traits associated with being male or female), gender identity (the psychological feeling of being male or female), and social gender roles, are distinct from sexual orientation (the cultural norms that define feminine and masculine behavior)

Commonly, sexual orientation is described as if it were the only personal trait that a person possessed, similar to biological sex, gender identity, or age. Because sexual orientation is defined in terms of connections with other people, this viewpoint is uncomplete. Individuals interact with people in a variety of ways to demonstrate their sexual orientation, such through holding hands or kissing. Hence, intimate relationships that satiate strongly felt needs for love, attachment, and intimacy are closely related to sexual orientation. These relationships also involve nonsexual physical love, common interests and ideals, support for one another, and continual dedication. Thus, sexual orientation is more than just a trait of an individualInstead, a person's sexual orientation determines the kind of people they are more likely to associate with in order to have the gratifying and successful romantic connections that are so important to many people's sense of self.

CHAPTER TWO

How do people find out if they are gay,lesbian or bisexual?

Current scientific and professional knowledge indicates that between middle childhood and the beginning of adolescence is when the main attractions that serve as the foundation for adult sexual orientation often emerge. Without any past sexual experience, these patterns of emotional, romantic, and sexual desire might develop. Whether lesbian, gay, bisexual, or straight, a person can be celibate and still be aware of their sexual orientation.

People who identify as lesbian, gay, or bisexual often have highly diverse sexual orientation-related experiences. Before they actively pursue relationships with other individuals, some people have long-standing knowledge of their sexual orientation as lesbian, gay, or bisexual. Before clearly defining their sexual orientation, some persons engage in sexual activity (with same-sex and/or othersex partners). Claiming a lesbian, gay, or bisexual identity may be a slow process because prejudice and discrimination make it difficult for many people to come to terms with their sexual orientation identities.

CHAPTER THREE

What causes a person to have a particular sexual orientation?

Regarding the precise causes of a person's development of a heterosexual, bisexual, gay, or lesbian orientation, scientists are divided. Although a lot of research has looked into the potential genetic, hormonal, developmental, social, and cultural impacts on sexual orientation, no results have been found that allow scientists to draw the conclusion that any one factor or variables cause sexual orientation. Many believe that both nature and nurture play intricate roles, and that most people have little to no control over their sexual orientation.

CHAPTER FOUR

What role do discrimination plays in the lives of LGBTQs?

Because of their sexual orientation, lesbian, gay, and bisexual people in the United States frequently face prejudice, discrimination, and violence. Over a large portion of the 20th century, there was widespread extreme prejudice against lesbians, homosexual men, and bisexual persons. Lesbian, homosexual, and bisexual persons were the focus of firmly held negative opinions among significant portions of the public, according to public opinion research conducted in the 1970s, 1980s, and 1990s. In recent years, the public has become more hostile to discrimination based on sexual orientation, yet animosity towards lesbians and gay men is still widespread in modern American culture. Bisexual prejudice appears to be prevalent at comparable levels. Bisexual people may actually experience discrimination from both heterosexual and some lesbian and gay people.

Discrimination based on sexual orientation can take various forms. The high incidence of harassment and violence aimed towards lesbian, gay, and bisexual people in American society is a direct result of severe anti-gay prejudice. Many studies show that verbal abuse and harassment are almost always experienced by lesbian, gay, and bisexual people. In addition, it indicates that discrimination against lesbian, gay, and bisexual people is still pervasive in both employment and housing.

Another area where prejudice and discrimination against lesbian, gay, and bisexual persons have had detrimental repercussions is the HIV/AIDS epidemic. The idea that HIV/AIDS was a "gay sickness" at the beginning of the pandemic contributed to the delay in addressing the significant social upheaval that AIDS would cause. The disease has disproportionately afflicted gay and bisexual men. Lesbian, gay, and bisexual persons have been stigmatised more because of the link of HIV/AIDS with homosexual and bisexual men and the false notion that all gay and bisexual men were infected.

CHAPTER FIVE

What is the psychological impact of discrimination?

Discrimination and prejudice affect people on a social and individual level. The common preconceptions of people in these groups represent prejudice and discrimination towards lesbians, gay men, and bisexual people on a social level. Although they are unfounded in fact, these prejudices nevertheless exist and are frequently invoked to justify the treatment of lesbian, gay, and bisexual persons differently. Stereotypical beliefs about lesbian, homosexual, and bisexual persons, for instance, are sometimes used to justify restrictions on employment prospects, parenthood, and relationship acceptance.

Such bias and discrimination may also have detrimental effects on an individual level, particularly if lesbian, gay, and bisexual people make an effort to hide or deny their sexual orientation. The social stigma against homosexuality is something that many lesbians and gay men learn to live with, but this pattern of prejudice can have detrimental repercussions on one's health and well-being. The impact of stigma on individuals and groups may be lessened or made worse by other qualities like race, ethnicity, religion, or handicap. Some lesbian, gay, and bisexual individuals might experience less stigma. For others, prejudice and discrimination may have a worsening effect because of their colour, sex, religion, disability, or other characteristics.

Lesbians and homosexual males frequently experience widespread prejudice, discrimination, and violence, which poses serious issues for their mental health. Lesbian, gay, and bisexual people experience significant stress due to anti-gay violence, sexual prejudice, and discrimination based on sexual orientation. Antigay attitudes and prejudice may make it difficult for lesbian, gay, and bisexual people to find social support, despite the fact that it is essential for stress management.

CHAPTER SIX

What is coming out and why is it important?

The term "coming out" is used to describe a variety of experiences that lesbian, gay, and bisexual people go through, including self-awareness of same-sex attraction, informing one or a few people about it, public disclosure of same-sex interest, and identification with the LGBT community. Due to the possibility of encountering prejudice and discrimination, many people are reluctant to come out. Some people prefer to remain anonymous, some elect to come out under certain restrictions, and some decide to come out in extremely public ways.

For lesbian, gay, and bisexual people, coming out is frequently a crucial psychological milestone. According to research, embracing one's sexual orientation and feeling good about it promotes better wellbeing and mental health. This integration frequently entails sharing one's identify with others, and it could also require engaging with the LGBT community. Discussing one's sexual orientation with others also makes it easier to access social support, which is essential for maintaining one's emotional and psychological well-being. Lesbians, gay men, and bisexual persons gain from having family, friends, and acquaintances in their lives, just like heterosexuals do. Hence, it is not shocking that lesbians and gay men who feel they must hide their sexual orientation report more frequently

Lesbians and homosexual men who are more openly gay have greater mental health issues than they do, and they can even have more physical health issues.

CHAPTER SEVEN

About coming out during the adolescence

Adolescence is a time when people start to build their independence and grow apart from their families and parents. Teenagers may explore during this time and struggle with their sexual desires. One of adolescence's typical developmental tasks is becoming conscious of one's sexual feelings. Teenagers' same-sex feelings or experiences might occasionally leave them unsure of their sexual orientation. With time and varying results for many people, this uncertainty seems to be fading

Some teenagers want to have same-sex relationships and act in that way, but they do not consider themselves to be lesbians, gays, or bisexual, perhaps due to the stigma attached to a nonheterosexual orientation. While some teenagers continue to be attracted to people of the same sex, they may refrain from sexual activity or choose to act in a heterosexual manner for varied periods of time. Due to the stigma surrounding same-sex attraction, many young people experience it for years before engaging in sexual activity with others of the same sex or admitting their feelings to others.

Some young people's exploration of same-sex inclinations results in the development of a lesbian, gay, or bisexual identity. Recognizing this identity may help some people put their confusion to rest. When parents and other adults provide these children with care, they are frequently able to lead happy, healthy lives and progress through the typical teenage development process. The fewer internal and external resources someone has when they accept their nonheterosexual identity, the younger they are likely to be. Teenagers who come out early therefore require extra support from their parents and others.

Teenagers who identify as lesbian, gay, or bisexual may be more prone to experience specific issues, such as bullying and unpleasant school experiences. These experiences are linked to unfavourable outcomes like suicidal ideation and high-risk behaviours like unprotected sex and drug and alcohol usage. On the other hand, many lesbian, gay, and bisexual youths don't seem to be at increased risk for physical or mental illness. Wherever issues arise, bias and discrimination in the environment have a strong correlation with those issues. Support from significant adults in the teen's life can act as a powerful counterbalance to prejudice and discrimination.

Assistance from the family, the classroom, and society at large helps to lower risk and promote healthy development. Young people require love and support, realistically high standards, and encouragement to interact with their classmates. Like any adolescents who thrive under pressure, lesbian, gay, and bisexual youth tend to be socially adept, have strong problem-solving abilities, a sense of autonomy and purpose, and have an optimistic outlook on the future.

In a similar vein, when some young people don't conform to traditional gender stereotypes, they are assumed to be lesbians, gays, or bisexual (i.e., the cultural beliefs about what is appropriate "masculine" and "feminine" appearance and behavior). These young people face bias and discrimination because it is assumed that they are lesbian, gay, or bisexual, regardless of whether they identify as heterosexual, lesbian, gay, or bisexual. School and social environments that do not accept discriminatory language and behaviour offer these young people the best help.

CHAPTER EIGHT

What age should a LGBTQ come out?

This question doesn't have a straightforward or definitive answer. For young people in various situations, coming out has distinct dangers and advantages. Some young individuals have families that openly and consistently embrace their sexual orientation; coming out may be less risky for these young people, even while they are still quite young. Coming out can be riskier for young people whose families are less accepting. All young people who come out may encounter prejudice, discrimination, or even violence in their educational institutions, social circles, places of employment, and religious settings. Supportive families, friends, and institutions of higher learning serve as vital barriers against the damaging effects of these encounters.

CHAPTER NINE

What is the nature of same-sex relationships?

According to research, many lesbians and homosexual men desire and maintain committed relationships. For instance, according to study results, between 40% and 60% of homosexual males and between 45% and 80% of lesbians are now in a romantic relationship. Furthermore, according to data from the 2000 U.S. Census, 594,391 of the 5.5 million unmarried couples who were living together in 2000 had partners of the same sex. The census numbers show that there are 301,026 male same-sex homes and 293,365 female same-sex households in the United States, despite the fact that they very probably underestimate the number of cohabiting same-sex couples.

Lesbian, gay, and bisexual stereotypes still exist today despite studies showing that they are inaccurate. One such stereotype is that lesbian and gay men's relationships are sad and dysfunctional. On measures of commitment and relationship satisfaction, same-sex and heterosexual couples have been found to be comparable to one another in studies.

Another myth is that lesbians, gay men, and bisexuals have unstable relationships. Nonetheless, research demonstrates that many lesbians and homosexual men develop long-lasting relationships despite social antagonism towards same-sex unions. For instance, according to study results, between 18 and 28 percent of gay couples and between 8 and 21 percent of lesbian couples have been living together for ten years or more. A valid argument might also be made that same-sex couples' stability might be improved if their partners had the same support and acknowledgement for their relationships as heterosexual couples do, i.e., the legal rights and obligations that come with marriage.

The belief that lesbian, gay, and bisexual couples have distinct values from heterosexual couples is a third prevalent myth. In fact, research has shown that same-sex cohabiting couples and heterosexual married couples exhibit striking similarities in the elements that affect relationship stability, commitment, and satisfaction.
The experiences of those who identify as bisexual have received far less research. These people will probably experience the same prejudice and discrimination as lesbian and gay couples if they are in a same-sex relationship. If they choose to come out as bisexual, they may experience some of the same prejudice and discrimination that lesbian and gay people do if they are in a heterosexual relationship. If they are not, their experiences may be quite similar to those of people who identify as heterosexual.

CHAPTER TEN

Can LGBTQs do a great job being a parent?

Many lesbians and gay men have children, and many more would like to. In the 2000 U.S. Census, at least one child under the age of 18 was living in the home for 33 percent of female same-sex couple households and 22 percent of male same-sex couple households. Many single lesbians and gay men are parents, and many same-sex couples are part-time parents to children whose principal residency is elsewhere, despite the lack of comparable data.

Several people have expressed worries regarding the welfare of the children in these homes as the social prominence and legal standing of lesbian and gay parents have grown. The majority of these inquiries are predicated on unfavourable stereotypes of lesbians and gay men. The majority of the studies on this subject focus on the question of whether children of lesbian and homosexual parents are less advantaged than those of heterosexual parents. The most typical queries and responses are as follows:

1.Do kids with gay and lesbian parents struggle with sexual identity more than kids with heterosexual parents?

Do these kids experience issues with gender identity or gender-role behaviour, for example? According to research, children of lesbian mothers develop their sexual and gender identities in a manner that is largely similar to that of children of heterosexual parents. This includes gender identity, gender-role behaviour, and sexual orientation. There aren't many research on children of gay fathers.

2.Do children of lesbian or gay parents experience difficulties with their own personal growth in areas other than sexual orientation?
Are children of lesbian or homosexual parents, for instance, more prone to mental illness, do they exhibit more behavioural issues, or are they less psychologically sound than other kids? Once more, research on personality, self-concept, and behaviour issues has found few variations between lesbian moms' children and heterosexual children. There aren't many research on children of gay fathers

3.Are kids of lesbian and gay parents more likely to struggle in social situations?
Will their peers bully them or otherwise treat them poorly, for instance? Once more, data suggests that children of lesbian and homosexual parents interact with classmates and adults in typical social ways. The findings of this study paint a picture of children of gay and lesbian parents who engage in social activities typical of their age group with peers, parents, family, and friends.

4.Are parents or friends or acquaintances of parents more likely to sexually abuse these kids?
The worry that children of lesbian or gay parents may be sexually abused by their parents or by their parents' gay, lesbian, or bisexual friends or acquaintances is not supported by any scientific research.

In conclusion, social research has demonstrated that the worries that are frequently voiced concerning children of lesbian and gay parents—concerns that are typically based on prejudice and stereotypes about homosexual people—are unwarranted. Generally, the evidence shows that the growth, adjustment, and general well-being of children of lesbian and gay parents are similar to those of children of heterosexual parents.

CHAPTER ELEVEN

Lesbian, gay, and bisexual people can be open about their sexual orientation while also taking the appropriate safety precautions if they want to lessen prejudice and discrimination. People can assess their own worldviews to see if any anti-gay prejudices are present. They can seek help from the lesbian, gay, bisexual, and transgender community as well as sympathetic heterosexuals.

Examining one's own reaction to anti-gay stereotypes and prejudice can assist heterosexual people fight discrimination and prejudice. They may make it a point to get to know lesbian, gay, and bisexual people, and they can collaborate with them and their communities to fight discrimination and prejudice. Those who identify as heterosexual are frequently in a position to ask other heterosexual people to think again about their prejudiced or discriminatory attitudes and behaviours. Allies who identify as heterosexual might support anti-discrimination laws that cover sexual orientation. They can make it such that exiting safely. Heterosexuals are given the chance to interact personally with openly homosexual people and to perceive their sexual orientation when lesbians, gay men, and bisexuals feel free to make public their sexual orientation

Prejudice consistently decreases when members of the majority group contact with members of a minority group, according to studies on prejudice, including prejudice towards LGBT people. Following this general trend, having direct contact with an openly gay person has been shown to have a significant impact on heterosexuals' acceptance of LGBT people. Those who have a close friend or family member who is gay or lesbian are much less likely to exhibit anti-gay beliefs, especially if the gay person has come out to the heterosexual person personally.

CONCLUSION

It's crucial to realise that, even though we often think of sexual orientation in terms of sexual attraction and romantic relationships, you don't necessarily need to have interacted sexually or been romantically involved with the type of person you find attractive in order to identify with that orientation. For instance, even if you've never dated a woman, you can identify as a lesbian if you identify as a woman and are attracted to other women. Even if you identify as bisexual, you might only have dated members of the gender you find attractive. Similar to that, you can choose to identify as asexual without ever having had a sexual relationship

Whatever your sexual orientation, you don't have to rush into any romantic or sexual experiences to prove it to yourself or to others.

www.ingramcontent.com/pod-product-compliance
Lightning Source LLC
Chambersburg PA
CBHW071554260726
48653CB00008BA/3181